Dangerous Storms

by Kristin Cashore

Scott Foresman
is an imprint of

Glenview, Illinois • Boston, Massachusetts • Chandler, Arizona
Upper Saddle River, New Jersey

Photographs

Every effort has been made to secure permission and provide appropriate credit for photographic material. The publisher deeply regrets any omission and pledges to correct errors called to its attention in subsequent editions.

Unless otherwise acknowledged, all photographs are the property of Pearson Education, Inc.

Photo locators denoted as follows: Top (T), Center (C), Bottom (B), Left (L), Right (R), Background (Bkgd)

3 ©Royalty-Free/Corbis; **4** ©Royalty-Free/Corbis; **6** ©Royalty-Free/Corbis; **7** Getty Images; **8** Hellen Sergeyeva/Shutterstock; **9** Getty Images; **10** Getty Images; **11** ©Royalty-Free/Corbis; **12** ©Royalty-Free/Corbis; **13** ©Royalty-Free/Corbis; **14** ©Royalty-Free/Corbis; **15** ©Royalty-Free/Corbis; **16** ©Royalty-Free/Corbis; **17** ©Royalty-Free/Corbis; **18** (T) ©Royalty-Free/Corbis, (B) Getty Images; **19** (T, C) ©Royalty-Free/Corbis.

ISBN 13: 978-0-328-52059-6
ISBN 10:   0-328-52059-4

Have you ever had your plans wrecked because of a storm? Maybe you were planning on going swimming, until lightning struck. Or perhaps you were planning on visiting a relative, until a blizzard hit.

No matter where you live, whether it is in the mountains, forest, desert, tropics, city, or country, at some time or another you will experience a storm. Storms happen everywhere. There is little that we can do to prevent them. But there's a lot that we can do to prepare for them!

Emergency crews help people find their belongings in the wreckage caused by storms.

Most storms pass by without any trouble. The sky turns **pitch** black, and it rains for an hour or so. You run out and jump in a few puddles, and then the sky clears. Or the snow falls quietly and **daintily** outside your window, as gentle as a **lullaby,** while you are falling asleep. In the morning, the world is beautiful and white, and you don't have to go to school! Sometimes a storm can make your day.

At other times, however, storms are not safe. Rain can cause flooding. Lightning can start fires. Winds can blow so hard and snow can fall so fast that it is not safe to go outside. And hurricanes or tornadoes can cause real **devastation.**

If you watch or listen to the weather forecast, you can be ready for even the most dangerous storm. If you are careful and **resourceful** during a storm, you are more likely to be safe. Every kind of storm brings different dangers. There are different safety tips to follow for each of nature's storms.

Thunderstorms

Thunderstorms are very common, especially during spring and summer. Thunderstorms can knock branches from trees. They can make messy puddles on street corners.

A thunderstorm may also have strong winds that knock over trees or bring down power lines. Sometimes hail falls. Often, hailstones are too small to cause any damage. But sometimes hail the size of golf balls drops from the sky. Hailstones this big can break windows and dent cars. Make sure never to go outside during a hailstorm!

A thunderstorm moves across this farm in the midwestern part of the country.

There are three other dangers that you should know about that are caused by thunderstorms. The first is lightning. Lightning happens during every thunderstorm. The second danger is flooding. The third is tornadoes. Whether a thunderstorm brings flooding or tornadoes depends upon many things, including where the storm happens.

These large hailstones can cause serious damage when they fall.

Thunder is harmless; it is only the sound that lightning makes. Lightning itself is what's dangerous.

Have you ever seen a tree split in half or **branded** black because it was hit by a lightning bolt? Lightning starts fires all around the world. It also hurts some people every year.

When lightning shoots from the sky to the ground, it chooses the shortest possible path. This means that it hits the highest object. That object could be a tall tree, a house, or a person standing in a flat field.

A lightning bolt can severely damage a tree.

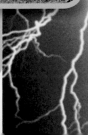

Protect Yourself from a Thunderstorm

- If you are outside, don't go into a shed, or wait under a large tree, or stand at the top of a hill.

- Don't carry or stand near anything made of metal.

- If possible, get inside a car. Cars are safe during storms with lightning.

- If you're in a field, crouch down on your knees and bend over. Do not lie down, because wet ground can conduct, or carry, electricity.

- If you are in the water, get out quickly, and move away from the beach.

- If you are inside, stay away from faucets, sinks, and tubs. They can conduct electricity.

- Don't use the phone, except in emergencies. Don't use anything with a cord that plugs into the wall. Lightning can pass to you through the cord.

If you can hear thunder, or if you can see veins of lightning in the sky, you are close to a storm. However, if you are careful, you can be safe from the dangers of lightning.

Flash Floods

Thunderstorms and rainstorms can cause terrible flash floods. Sometimes, when it rains very hard, there is no time for the ground to absorb the rain. The water begins to move over the land. It sweeps into gullies and ditches. Within hours or even minutes, the water turns into a raging river that can wreck anything in its path. In the United States, more people die every year from flooding than from lightning or tornadoes.

Flash floods can happen even if it is not raining in your town. It is a good idea to plan and prepare in order to be safe from flash floods.

Flash floods can cause many problems. This road was closed because of a flash flood.

Protect Yourself from a Flash Flood

- Pay attention to weather forecasts. Know when you are at risk.

- Have a plan for where to go if there is flooding in your area. If officials tell you to leave your house and go someplace safe, then do what they say.

- Store water and food that doesn't need to be cooked or kept cold, in case you lose power.

- Keep a first-aid kit, flashlight, and radio handy.

- Do not go outside to watch the water rise.

- If you are outside, move away from ditches and stream beds. Move to higher ground.

- Remember that if it is raining, there may be lightning. If you are outside, keep your lightning safety tips in mind.

Always take the risks of a flash flood seriously. Following a few simple rules could save your life.

Tornadoes

A tornado is made up of air that is spinning very fast. The air spins itself into the shape of a funnel. Tornadoes happen most often in the plains of North America, between the Rocky Mountains and the Appalachian Mountains. Tornadoes tend to happen during spring and summer.

The wind inside a tornado can spin at three hundred miles per hour, or more. A tornado can lift cars into the air and tear trees out of the ground. It can pull roofs from houses, even if the houses are well **constructed.** Tornadoes can be strong enough to send glass and wood flying through the air.

When a tornado touches the ground, it can cause severe damage.

Protect Yourself from a Tornado

- Pay attention to tornado warnings. When you hear a warning, move quickly.

- If you have a storm shelter, go to it.

- If you don't have a storm shelter, go into the basement and get under something strong, such as a staircase. This is to protect you from flying and falling objects.

- If you don't have a basement, go to a windowless part of your house, such as a hallway or closet.

- Stay away from windows. They may shatter.

- If you are in a mobile home or a car, leave and go to someplace safer.

- If you are in the open, lie down in a low area and cover your head with your arms. If possible, find something to hold on to.

- Know your school's tornado safety plan.

If you hear a tornado warning, don't waste time. As with flash floods, a good plan makes all the difference.

Hurricanes

Like thunderstorms, hurricanes bring flooding and dangerous winds. A hurricane starts as a tropical storm in the waters over the Atlantic or eastern Pacific Oceans. It can create huge waves and heavy rains. The storm is called a hurricane if it produces winds of more than seventy-three miles per hour. If a hurricane moves onto land, its winds, rain, and waves can destroy houses, cars, and trees.

During a hurricane, the ocean level rises as much as twenty-five feet. This creates waves that can sink ships and wash away houses. These waves are called a storm surge.

As a hurricane spreads out over the ocean, it causes enormous waves.

Protect Yourself from a Hurricane

- Know if your house is in the path of the storm surge. Plan where you will go to escape the storm surge.

- Pay attention to the weather forecast, and leave if you are told to do so.

- Before the storm, put boards or tape on your windows. Get flashlights and a radio. Remove small items from your yard. They could become dangerous flying objects.

- Stay inside during the hurricane, away from the windows.

- Don't be fooled by the calm in the middle of the hurricane, called the eye. The Sun may shine inside the eye, but the storm still rages all around it.

- If you live near the shore, go inland.

There is nothing you can do to stop the storm surge. If you live near the shore, plan to move far away from the water during a hurricane. You can avoid the storm surge if you act quickly.

Blizzards

During snowstorms and blizzards, roads and walkways become icy and slippery for drivers and walkers. Heavy snow can pull down power lines. If a house is without electricity for a long time, it will become cold and the water pipes may freeze and burst. During the worst blizzards, heavy, wet snow can pull down trees and make the roofs of houses cave in. People can leave home and never find their way back because they are blinded by the thick snow. Drivers trapped in a blizzard may be in danger if they do not have food, water, blankets, and a first-aid kit in their cars.

After a blizzard, snow-filled roads must be plowed to be made safe for cars.

Protect Yourself During a Blizzard

- Pay attention to the weather forecast, and plan ahead.

- Don't travel by car, unless you must.

- Store flashlights, candles, water, and food that doesn't need to be cooked or kept cold.

- Keep blankets handy. The electricity may go off, and you will need to stay warm.

- Have a battery-operated radio. Buy extra batteries.

- During a very bad storm, do not go outside unless you are attached to the house by a lifeline, or you may get lost.

- If you must go out during a blizzard, wear many layers of clothing. Try to wear wool and a wind-resistant coat.

A winter storm can be very dangerous if you are not ready for it. Be smart during winter storm season—prepare yourself.

We can't do anything to stop storms from coming. **Thieving** nature has a mind of her own. She can take our houses, our trees, and our property, and do what she wants with them! However, scientists have learned how to predict some storms. They can warn us when storms might be coming. It is our job to prepare for storms so that we reduce our chances of getting hurt when they hit.

This devastation was caused by a tornado. It took years for people to clean up their homes and get their lives in order.

Tornado

Flash Flood

Hurricane

19

Glossary

branded *v.* marked by burning.

constructed *adj.* put together.

daintily *adv.* with delicate beauty.

devastation *n.* the act of laying waste, destroying.

lullaby *n.* a soft song sung to put a baby to sleep.

pitch *n.* a thick, black, sticky substance made from tar.

resourceful *adj.* good at thinking of ways to do things.

thieving *adj.* likely to steal.

veins *n.* natural channels through which water flows, or the tubes that carry blood through your body.